The Birth of Bhairava

ALSO BY DIPA SANATANI

The Guardians of the Lore Trilogy
The Little Light
The Heart of Shiva
The Prophetess of Dharma

Fiction
A Thousand Names
Illuminator
Divinely Destined
Sacrifice

Poetry
Oneness
The River Empress
Ink Stained Soul
Kingfisher

Creative Non-Fiction
The Merchant of Stories

The Birth of Bhairava

Dipa Sanatani

twinn swan
est. 2019

National Library Board, Singapore Cataloguing in Publication Data

Name(s): Sanatani, Dipa.
Title: The birth of Bhairava / Dipa Sanatani.
Description: Singapore : Twinn Swan, [2026]
Identifier(s): ISBN 978-981-94-4923-1 (hardcover) | 978-981-94-4924-8 (paperback) | 978-981-94-4925-5 (ebook)
Subject(s): LCSH: Belief and doubt--Fiction. | Spirituality--Fiction.
Classification: DDC S823--dc23

The Book Cover is designed by Dipa Sanatani.

TWINN SWAN
Singapore
www.dipasanatani.com

For Sri Ardhanarishvara

The Lord Whose Half is Woman

Invocation to Lord Shiva

Verse in Devanāgarī

प्रदीप्तरत्नोज्ज्वलकुण्डलायै स्फुरन्महापन्नगभूषणाय ।

शिवान्वितायै च शिवान्विताय नमः शिवायै च नमः शिवाय ॥

Transliteration

Pradīptaratnojjvala-kuṇḍalāyai

Sphuran-mahāpannaga-bhūṣaṇāya

Śivānvitāyai ca Śivānvitāya

Namaḥ Śivāyai ca Namaḥ Śivāya

English Translation

Salutations to the Divine Couple

To Her whose earrings shine with the blaze of radiant gems,

To Him adorned with the luminous, mighty serpent,

To Her who is ever united with Śiva,

And to Him who is ever one with Her

salutations to Śivā and to Śiva

-Verse 8 of *Ardhanārīśvara Stotram by Sri Adi Śaṅkarācārya.*

Preface

Across religious traditions, the soul's separation from the divine—manifesting as egoic limitation, ignorance or sin—forms the core narrative of the human condition, inherent to creation's purposeful design for cosmic play and spiritual evolution.

The infinite Oneness contracts into finite forms to ultimately unveil its True Self through self-effort and divine grace. This primordial exile, termed as the 'divine play' or 'fall into multiplicity', enables free will and experiential growth through duality and reunion.

The primary focus of this book is to explore the concept of *anava mala*—the soul's primordial ignorance—as understood in Shaiva Siddhanta philosophy. *Anava mala* is the soul's experience of separation from the Living Truth of its divinity, giving rise to a fundamental sense of isolation and ego that binds it to the cycle of birth, death, and rebirth. This perception of separation is an ingrained impediment that obscures the perception of the True Self.

Shakti's journey reveals the sovereign power of the Divine Feminine and illuminates the path of transcendence for those who seek the Living Truth within. Through her death and rebirth as Sati and Parvati, this work unveils a core truth: *anava mala* yields only to the purifying fire of *tapasya*—the gradual dissolution of the ego that opens the way for Shiva's grace.

The philosophy in this book draws inspiration from the Pauskara Agama—Vidya Pada, a Shaiva scripture illuminating Shiva's metaphysical principles and the highest knowledge for spiritual realisation. This ancient text, part of the revelatory Agama tradition, guides aspirants through cosmology, consciousness, and union with the divine.

By drawing upon timeless lessons espoused in the Puranas and the Agamas, this book draws on philosophical inquiry and lived experience to illuminate how *anava mala* shapes the human condition and how transcendence of this separation is the soul's final goal.

May this work of prose inspire reflection towards the realisation of eternal union with the divine.

Om Namah Shivaya. Om Shakti.

Contents

Part 1
Anava Mala

Obscuration

1

Salutations to Lord Bhairava, the Fierce One

Om Bhairavāya Namaḥ

The incarnation of Sati had continued to echo somewhere within Him, faded by time, but still burning within.

He had memorialised her as a frozen flame buried deep beneath the endless and eternal landscape of Himalayan silver.

Sometimes, when the mountain lay half-buried in mist, I thought I heard the faint breath of her memory.

In the vast stillness of His solitude, as He sat solemnly in his meditation, He was shaping Her return, unseen and unhurried, through the very womb of the earth.

Time unfolded as an illusion, for all lifetimes arose simultaneously in the Sacred Silence where past, present and future are already known.

Many millennia passed before I understood that His meditation was a remembrance which stretched across all the ages—the vow of a love that lives beyond death—waiting, waiting, waiting—to resurrect itself.

I am waiting for you.

Om.

2

Homage to the Master of the Spirits

Om Bhūtanāthāya Namaḥ

O Shiva, my voice rises inwardly, as the ancient echo of my soul abruptly awakens.

Before the unparalleled vastness of your Universe, I finally permit the armour of my mind to fall.

I am Nandi. Your *vahana*, your vehicle, your eternal companion and the Guardian of the Gate. I am your *bhakta*, your *siddha*, the foremost of all your disciples.

In the infinite vastness of Your being dwells a joy and a bliss beyond my current state of comprehension.

You are Shiva. Timeless, endless, deathless, beyond birth and beyond death.

You burned the citadels of arrogance and the demigod of desire, yet no flame can ever vanquish your mercy.

O Lord whose stillness outlasts the stars, you hold within you all that words can never even hope to name—power and beauty, wisdom and knowledge, the futility and fullness of every wish.

You are Shiva, my *Mahadeva*.

3

Salutations to the Soul of All Existence

Om Bhūtātmanē Namaḥ

You, O Mahadeva, drank the poison the world could not bear, and let it stain your throat so creation could continue.

In Your blueness, I see the endlessness of a love that gives infinitely of itself without measure.

Your hair burns with the dusk's tawny light and from it the crescent moon smiles gently like an old companion reminiscing about the cyclical nature of time.

Around your body lies the calm of the wilderness: the hide of the tiger and the quiet breathing of beasts that have forgotten their ancient enmity.

All life yields under the gaze of your eternal presence.

Let me remain here, in this sacred closeness that dissolves all boundaries of self, yet sets my spirit blazing with new life.

4

Salutations to the Source that Brings All Beings into Existence

Om Bhūtabhāvanāya Namaḥ

For the entire duration of Time, the expanse known as eternity, He sat thus, burdened and buried deep within the vast solitude of His own being.

The snows rose and fell, veiling His human form.

The stars circled their countless rounds and yet He remained unmoved and untouched by time or change.

Upon His head, the frost mingled with his matted locks.

Around His neck, Vasuki, *Nagaraja*, Sovereign of all the Serpents, stood guard in benefaction.

My Lord, my beloved Mahadeva, whom I adored with all my heart, had turned inward, beyond name and form.

No sound of the three worlds could reach where His consciousness now dwelt.

The most ancient of all the rivers murmured His name as they ceased to flow from the mountain's breast, for there was naught but motionless silence to carry down to the earthly realm.

Even the wind that touched Him lost its restlessness and grew still.

He had retreated to the heart of all things—the hidden realm where dissolution and regeneration danced as one.

None dared to approach Him, not even me.

I took my station as the Guardian of Mount Kailasa when my Lord retreated from the worlds to recover from his grief.

My sole duty and desire was to stand guard at the mountain as his *vahana* till He arose once more, to destroy and regenerate the three worlds.

Despite the depth of his stillness, I have faith that one day He will arise and dance again.

Who are we… Who are any of us… without faith?

5

Hail to the Knower of All Fields and Realms

Om Kṣetrajñāya Namaḥ

There is no Shiva without Shakti. There is no Shakti without Shiva.

Who amongst us—Divine or mortal—is powerful enough to circumvent what has no choice but to be?

No, no… Fate is not a rigid decree.

The intervals granted to us—the pauses before destiny's final arrival—carry the burden of patience and postponement.

It is here that the truest freedom resides. It lies in how we choose to prepare for the burdens life inevitably bestows upon us.

Do we stumble through life weighed down by resentment, scattering bitter seeds for the journeys yet to come?

Or do we lift our eyes, placing each footstep with the detached grace that comes from foreknowledge and acceptance?

The tale of Sati is one I will not forget, nor will the timeless mountains that cradled her when she rose anew.

There is no Shakti without Shiva. There is no Shiva without Shakti.

Om.

6

Homage to the Guardian Protector of the Sacred Space

Om Kṣetrapālāya Namaḥ

Age after age passed like the slow unfolding of a lotus. The ages arose, heralding the birth, death and rebirth of Bhairava, Father Time.

The gods grew anxious for the Divine Beings hungered to restore the great balance between realms.

Then, one day, I felt it—the first tremor of a new stirring upon the sacred mountain.

The air changed, scented with life once more.

She had taken birth again—as the daughter of the very mountain that sheltered him in His solitude.

The wind carried Her laughter… and even in His state of samadhi, something within Him seemed to hear her.

7

Salutations to the Giver of the Field

Om Kṣetradāya Namaḥ

The ancient goddess had returned, her timeless essence manifesting in a new human vessel.

Sati had been shed; Parvati had materialised.

It was on the night of the eclipsed moon—when the world hid from Rahu's grasp amid the deepest obscuration of *anava mala*—that she first sensed His presence.

Her spirit remembered Him for her Time had come once more.

I heard her plea and her supplication, her yearning for her Lord.

"The truth I have sought through countless forms and faces—as I called out to you again and again under the magenta shadow of the lunar eclipse, chanting your thousand names three times over—is, on this eclipsed night, one hundred thousand times more powerful than the ordinary day.

"O Shiva, in this raw nearness, may I find refuge and renewal, sheltered by your infinite embrace as I surrender to the yearning that calls me home.

"Your presence fills the vast space within me—compassionate and tender for you are the Destroyer of Darkness and the Protector of Dharma.

"The penance of tonight unveils the obscurity, the *anava mala,* before me fully now. You are the eternal beginning and the still breath between all beginnings.

"I am no longer Sati. I am now Parvati. You are Shiva. My *Mahadeva.*"

Part 2
Sati

Truth

8

Salutations to the Warrior Lord

Om Kṣatriyāya Namaḥ

Long before Sati even neared the flames of her father's *yajna*—that fateful sacrificial gathering—Shiva's divine sight had already traced the full, tragic arc of what was destined to be.

The trepidation was old in Shiva's eyes, a memory of a future scene forecasted and foretold well before its arrival.

The course was already set.

He saw, with perfect clarity, the sharp sting of shame that would pierce Sati's heart, knowing it was all an inevitability—a wound destined to be delivered even before the goddess took mortal birth.

Sati would venture forth
to her father's house
with unguarded innocence,
carrying within her
the futile hope
that a father's love
might triumph
over the fractures
wrought by self-interest,
ignorance and arrogance.

Though He, the Mahadeva, the all-knowing, counselled caution, He did not obstruct her path, for even the gods themselves cannot deny or deter the cosmic law.

Her fierce love
Her loyalty

Her dignity
were destined
to collide with
the cold arrogance
of her father.

The unbearable
shame of Sati
would awaken
an inner fire
no earthly force
could ever hope
to quench.

Yet in that foreknowledge,
there was no relief,
only the throbbing of inevitability,
the terrible burden of witnessing
the agony of the Beloved,
but knowing fully
that one simply cannot
alter the tide of fate's fury.

In the moments before the self-sacrifice, the irreversible change on the horizon hung thick with foreboding: the ancient quietude of a blizzard born of both cosmic justice and deeply personal pain.

9

I Bow to the Luminous One, the Radiant Sovereign

Om Virāje Namaḥ

To know the precise trajectory of the arrow does not soften the agony when the bowstring is released.

To foresee it and to live through it are two separate things.

Even before Sati crossed the threshold to attend her father's sacrifice, He foresaw the shadow of sorrow that it would cast upon her soul.

The fire was inevitable. It could neither be circumvented nor averted.

To sit upon the peak
to allow his Beloved
to walk into the flames
to enforce the cosmic law
even upon His own heart
required a resignation
deeper than
any human sorrow.

Mahadeva must have known of the precise measure of purification it would bring.

It is the acceptance of destiny, where even the Divine must endure the script already known, feeling, wholeheartedly, the wrench of separation even as He remains the source of all things.

10

Hail to the One Who Dwells in the Cremation Ground

Om Śmaśānavāsine Namaḥ

At the gate of Kailash, I sat in a silent vigil, my breath tethered to the stillness of my Lord. Shiva sat unmoving, yet in the depths of that quietude, the heartbeat of the earth had already foretold the trembling truth to those who dared to listen.

The moments preceding the *yajna*—when all that would unfold was already known in the hidden realm before entering Time—there was a pregnant pause: silent, weighted, and distinguished by its solemn and sacred inevitability.

Sati believed that in the blood tie—and in her love for Shiva—there still remained a chance for reconciliation. She held onto the hope that Daksha's scorn might be softened by truth.

She stepped forward, unarmed except for optimism—the fragile faith that a father's love might still choose to heal the egoic sense of separation carved by self-interest, ignorance and arrogance.

My Mahadeva, my Shiva, whose vision pierced the veils of illusion, continued to counsel caution.

Do not go.

He had foreseen the living flame awaiting her at the *yajna* and yet He did not, could not, restrict her movement.

Sati's will was unyielding. *Daksha is my father and I am his daughter.*

She walked alone into the gathering where her own humiliation awaited her.

Do not go.

Daksha is my father and I am his daughter.

11

Salutations to the Lord Who Devours the Illusions of the Flesh

Om Māṁsāśine Namaḥ

Within the perfection
of his meditation
the future
played out in his mind
long before it occurred.

Far away from the *yajna,*
upon the Kailasa Mountains,
unwanted and uninvited

my Lord sat utterly still.

Even before the consuming conflagration ravaged his Beloved, Shiva discerned the true purpose of the *yajna*, the sacrificial fire.

The fate of
the Divine Daughter
was bound
to the fatal necessity
brought on
by her father Daksha's
sense of separation.

The story between father and daughter had reached the chapter that demanded its inevitable and irreversible end.

Do not go, he cautioned. *Do not go*.

Do not return to your father's house. You are no longer welcome there.

12

Homage to the Fierce One Holding the Emblems of Mortality

Om Kharparāśine Namaḥ

When Sati entered Daksha's hall, he neither rose nor spoke her name. The warmth of a father's embrace was deliberately withheld, for his was a cold silence marking his rejection of her presence.

Daksha's *yajna* was a grand spectacle of decadence and extravagance rooted in his own egoic need for external validation.

Words arranged like serpents slid through the air—insults directed not just towards her, but to her Lord and her very soul.

You are not welcome here.

Am I not your daughter?

The guests gathered were an echo chamber of cruel whispers, further tearing away at the delicate bond once upheld by blood ties and family honour.

To the discerning eye, it was all a display created to exalt himself and snub Sati and Shiva.

For Daksha, the *yajna* was a platform erected solely for dominance. It was the theatre wherein his rank would be exalted, his authority declared unassailable, and his reputation permitted to burn with a hostile lustre.

That his self-aggrandisement required the degradation and deprecation of his own daughter's was, in his estimation, a negligible prerequisite for power.

Sati was suddenly reminded of the counsel which she had been provided.

Do not go.

Unable to bear the double agony—her own father's venomous rejection and the wound inflicted on her Beloved—Sati finally understood.

As she gazed into the furnace of the sacrificial fire, her conviction that a father's love for his daughter might bridge the gulf carved by pride and calculation disappeared.

Do not return to your father's house. You are no longer welcome there.

Alas, it was too late to turn back the trajectory of Fate's tide.

13

I Bow to the Destroyer of Memory

Om Smarāntakāya Namaḥ

Fate has never paid any heed to caution. It wraps its tendrils around you, refusing to alter the trajectory of its tide.

Love's tangled web remains forever undeterred by fear or doubt.

Sati walked into this tempest, moving forward with a heart brimming with love and loyalty rather than the cold and calculated strategies of power.

The admonition she had received to retreat was rendered moot.

The Truth is: she had not simply ignored the counsel. She had been made deaf to it by the clamour of her own fate. Her destiny was a fixed certainty—one that admitted no external voice. Each step was a deliberate sealing of her fate, preparing herself for the expiating fire—the sole, necessary means of purchasing her soul's absolution.

When Sati stepped across the boundary of Daksha's *yajna*, the altar flame did not waver, but burned with a strange, impossible stillness, as though it were a witness frozen in dread.

The truth, which was veiled to all the participants, was that Sati was neither a demure daughter of Daksha begging for approval nor an ardent devotee of Shiva paralysed by pride.

Truth is forever innocent to the world's cunning and scheming ways for Truth knows that life is fragile and fleeting.

Sati was the embodiment of Parashakti—the great primal energy—made mortal, incarnating to fulfil the fulcrum of cosmic law.

She had taken birth to be a carefully and precisely measured spark destined to ignite the collapse of a false and exhausted order.

She remembered His words.

Do not go.

She had not had a choice. Not truly.

When the divinity within is obscured by *anava mala,* the soul is veiled by the primal sense of separation. All notion of choice or free will becomes a cruel deception, for the spirit perceives the universe only through the limitations of obscuration.

14

Homage to the One Who Consumes the Crimson Nectar of Sacrifice

Om Raktapāya Namaḥ

Around the gathering, rumour after rumour disintegrated like dry leaves under a cold wind.

The crowd's murmurs blurred into a distant hum, an echo swallowed by the roar of her inner fire.

Voices and whispers
lingered upon the wind

urging Daksha
to stay clear
of the gathering storm

Fan not the living flames of this fire.

Daksha remained undaunted and undeterred as he continued on in his quest for self-destruction.

Deluded Daksha… Delusional Daksha… Delirious Daksha…

His words fell like jagged stones, each syllable cracking the brittle air.

His footsteps
circled the yajna
as a predator
perfectly poised
to pounce on
his chosen victim.

The intense fervour of

his false judgment

continued

to dictate his actions.

Within him, the separation had congealed into a brutal, unyielding contour; yet within her final exhalation, the dividing boundaries dissipated, melting as mist before a nascent sun.

Fan not the flames of this living fire.

The flames of the *yajna* leapt higher than the altar, yet their heat was nothing compared to the fire which was burning in Sati's chest.

She began to move as a living torch given form—her Living Truth, her essence reaching beyond flesh and bone—burned through the tapestry of falsehood and lies.

Where his pride sought to chain and claim her spirit, an unseen light danced in her eyes—an inner ember glowing through ash, promising worlds undone and remade.

Her body was consumed, vanishing into the Truth. The silent anthem of her spirit ascended unfettered as a covenant forged beyond the constraints of grief and earthly pride.

Daksha's damaged ego—seated on a throne of brittle commands—trembled beneath the weight of her act of self-sacrifice.

The ego must be eradicated, for Bhairava's birth can neither be delayed nor denied.

When the fervent essence of her inner fire ignited to reclaim her transient mortal vessel, it constituted both a termination and an inauguration.

What ultimately remained was not grief, not truly, but rather, the first omen that Father Time would finally be born.

15

Salutations to the Lord Who Consumes Poison

Om Pānapāya Namaḥ

Her resolve was absolute. Sati's hand steadied as she reached deep within to summon the eternal, living flame that smouldered in her core. The fire erupted—a blinding, white heat that claimed her entirely, rising to seize its throne of sovereignty.

Sati had returned into the timeless source from which she had emerged, a river folding once more back into the sea. Her act of self-sacrifice was a purging, a cleansing fire that severed the transient tie tethering her to suffering, pain and falsehood.

Flesh and bone gave way, but what broke to burn was far older: the fragile bond between a father and a daughter, a rupture rooted in the patriarch's pride and blind refusal to see the Truth.

A brutal silence fell over the yajna. The air hummed, charged by an invisible fracture. The expanding rift, born of arrogance, fear, and a power that was already crumbling, was a scream waiting to be heard.

Time and again, the hubris of Daksha's ego unsettled the delicate scales of dharma, each imbalance sending ripples through the cosmos.

His contempt struck like a hammer against the bell of fate, the clang echoing far beyond mortal ears.

The chapter with his daughter closed with smoke curling into the sky.

From deep within his samadhi, Shiva's voice brushed through the silence, a whisper carrying across realms.

You are Sati. You are the Living Truth. Om.

16

Hail to the Accomplished and Perfected One

Om Siddhāya Namaḥ

In that irrevocable instant, Sati's temporal mortal identity shattered. The roles of daughter, wife, consort, and unwelcome guest were all consumed by the sovereignty of her inner flame.

The shame Daksha inflicted upon the incarnation of Shakti as Sati vanished instantaneously, replaced by a clarity—an upending reality—that was both terrible and unalterable.

Her departure was predetermined by fate, a force known as Divine Will that neither falters nor fears in the face of pitiless adversity.

When her temporal incarnation as Sati dissolved into pure energy, the first act of cosmic dissolution was complete.

Her departure from the mortal coil bestowed upon her by her temporary parents left behind a luminous truth. She was not a woman lost, but the bearer of a necessary cataclysm, born to fulfil a cosmic law far greater than the attachment her death undid.

Part 3
Birth

Avatara

17

Homage to the Bestower of Spiritual Powers

Om Siddhidāya Namaḥ

The Earth paused to witness the turning of a great wheel.

High above, the stars traced indifferent circles, but below, the tremor of the broken law startled the most ancient of the shadow spirits.

At Kailash's peak, I, the Guardian of the Gate, felt the new breath of irreversible change once again brush against my being.

The crescent on His brow dimmed beneath the blaze of His third eye.

When the tidings of Sati's self-immolation reached Kailasa, the earth under which Shiva mediated drew its breath in fear.

The Lord rose from the solitude of His silence, His body shivering like the sea before the tsunami.

A seismic tear fell through the fabric of existence as the Lord's primal scream split the sky open.

Shiva did not weep. He unleashed.

18

Homage to the One Worshipped by the Accomplished Masters

Om Siddhisevitāya Namaḥ

Who dares sign the ledger of disgrace with the complicity of their silence? Who dares to draw from the account that creates strife and suffering, failing to see the exact price recorded against their name?

The balance sheet of fate awaits its settlement.

Destiny, fate, kismet, wraps its tender tendrils around both gods and mortal alike.

Shiva would never again foresee the bright and final leap of His beloved for what he had foreseen had come to pass.

He witnessed, from his eternal abode in Kailasa, the one act of self-sacrifice required to purify the accumulated egoic darkness of the world.

From that stern resolve—born of witnessing her humiliation—Bhairava emerged, a shadow loosening from the heart of stillness. His eyes raged like embers for he carried the indignation of the oppressed and the innocent.

As the shadow of unjust family betrayal gathered strength, Shiva emerged as the fierce guardian god, a being born of searing, protective rage.

Unlike the other gods, Bhairava was born bare and unadorned, springing from the cosmic law that governs all.

His *avatara* as Bhairava heralded the birth of retributory justice striding through the twilight where darkness clawed at the world's seams.

That sanctuary was the point where solitary devotion encountered the vast cosmic architecture, and in that meeting, all distress was transmuted into unbound liberation.

19

I Bow to the Reality Beyond the Flesh

Om Kaṅkālāya Namaḥ

I saw Him seated, unmoved, eyes deep as time itself, the weight of cosmic balance pressing silently upon His infinite consciousness.

Around Him, the threads of fate pulled taut, timorous with a force both wrathful and just.

In that grief-stricken stillness, the strands of His matted hair loosened and fell. He would not permit this injustice to remain unacknowledged and unaccounted for.

I watched as a figure took shape in the gathering dusk, silent and unyielding as a shadow dancing against the dimming light.

The tide ordained by the eternal dharma was no unexpected eruption of anger. The broken yajna, the shattered vows, the proud defiance of a fallen king—they all converged into this moment.

The world would reclaim its balance, the sacred cycle restoring and reclaiming itself with relentless certainty.

Bhairava was born as a retributory turning of justice: a force summoned to set right what ignorance and arrogance had undone.

As each thread touched the earth, the soil pulsed with a new life—raw, fierce and inevitable.

As Bhairava rose, so too did the knowledge in my heart: the living flame of self-sacrifice was the birth of what is yet to be.

20

Salutations to the Pacifier of Time

Om Kālaśamanāya Namaḥ

"Look upon her," Daksha commanded, gesturing with a dismissive sweep that demanded the attention of everyone present. "She carries my blood, yet she has publicly discarded my name, my purpose, and my protection for the ash and wild silence of Shiva. She is *nothing* without me and yet she dares to defy me. Now she is a mirror of her own poor judgment and nothing more."

Around her, the murmurs of the attendees were distant, cackling and cold, isolating her in a spotlight of shame.

The helplessness she once felt was gone, replaced by a devastating clarity: her body, born of his blood, was the last thing tying her to him. And that, she knew with absolute certainty, had to be forfeited.

He had cast her out with a public, brutal erasure, and she, his daughter, would now answer that erasure with an absolute negation of her own.

Daksha, magnificent on his high dais, did not merely speak—he performed. He had carefully orchestrated this moment. He leaned forward, his gaze dismissing and dissecting his daughter as his voice calibrated to carry the cold finality of a false and flawed judgment.

This was Daksha's temporary triumph. His words did not merely damage the bond they had shared. It had snapped and severed it.

Sati saw the thin, satisfied curl of his lip—the confirmation that this humiliation was a determined and deliberate act of erasure.

All that remained was a cold, magnificent judge who cared more for his ego than for his own blood.

In that moment, the father she had adored—the one whose approval, affection and adoration she had sought—vanished. Waves upon waves of humiliation crashed down upon her, yet beneath them, the light she carried within did not dim—it brightened.

21

Homage to the Embodiment of All Moments and Units of Time

Om Kalākāṣṭhatanave Namaḥ

Silence fell heavy as the heavens darkened.

From the stillness of Kailash
where my Lord had witnessed all
His wrath rose like thunder
emanating in Bhairava.

Bhairava strode into the sacrificial ground, unyielding and unstoppable.

He emerged from
the grief of Shiva
dark and terrible
a black as annihilation itself
for he emerged from
the depths of night.

The fire that once honoured the *yajna* now turned against its priests. The proud ceremony crumbled to dust and decay beneath the unbearable weight of Truth.

His eyes burned with fury
for in his hands
the terrible sword of justice
sang the song of severance.

The proud Daksha, caught in the plateau of silence before the storm, felt his arrogance shatter as Bhairava's blade struck through the Truth.

The head of the haughty self-proclaimed lord fell, rolling into the sacred flames that devoured both ego and illusion.

Daksha's severed head burned, his arrogance finally vanquished beneath the fire of the Truth he had dared to defy.

22

I Bow to the Divine Poet, the Wise One

Om Kavaye Namaḥ

I saw the world still, as if holding its breath, awaiting the retribution that would echo through all realms.

There is no Shiva without Shakti. There is no Shakti without Shiva.

In the moment Sati was consumed by her inner flame, the very essence of Shiva was irrevocably altered.

Beside Him, I bore witness to a sorrow that eclipsed all human measure, for that grief was no longer sorrow: it had reshaped itself into divine judgment.

The weight of her death became a force that destroyed the boundary between the tender husband and the unforgiving cosmic lawgiver.

He had become Bhairava, Protector of Dharma.

It was the birth of a new Shiva: one who would now carry the unbearable weight of love lost and whose embodiment of divine justice would not tolerate arrogance.

Bhairava was the eternal emanation to the deeper indignation beneath his divine calm and the fire that would obliterate all that dared to defy cosmic order.

23

I bow to the Lord of Inner Vision

Om Trinetrāya Namaḥ

The soundless silence was shattered only by the faint hiss of dying embers from the sacrificial fire.

Low and awed whispers drifted from the stunned gods. No one had expected that this would ensue in the aftermath of the sacrifice.

The sword Bhairava raised embodied the living essence of all who had experienced repeated and rampant humiliation and indignation at the hands of a tyrant. The sharpness of the edge pulsed with the destiny of cosmic balance, its steel lustrous with the eventual inevitability of justice.

With a decisive and deliberate—immaculate and unwavering—stroke, the blade fell.

Flesh, bone and ego were severed in a single stroke.

The scent of burnt offerings mingled with the metallic tang of judgment, sealing the fate that had been long decreed.

Fan not the flames of this fire.

A peculiar hush filled the space as Daksha's head separated from his body—his defiance and false power finally destroyed.

This moment, an act of violence, was a solemn reordering, a justice dealt with a sacred precision that only Bhairava, as the embodiment of Shiva's justice and cosmic order, could deliver.

I, his disciple and witness, moved in awe of the tireless certainty of divine law made incarnate.

24

Praise to the Lord with Infinite Vision

Om Bahunetrāya Namaḥ

Shiva's body swayed to a rhythm beyond mercy or madness. The matted hair that once framed his face fell away, stars igniting in its place.

The dance was the turning of the Eternal Wheel: a retributive reality written into the fabric of reality itself.

It was destruction, yes, but destruction as mercy, retribution and inevitability.

Through Shiva's sorrow-fuelled rage, the broken order was purged, and from its ashes, the path for renewal was made manifest.

To stand witness was to behold both the end and the beginning entwined in the same singular dance.

Each step shook the earth and rent the sky. Each gesture and each moment destroyed the damaged threads of fate woven with the silk of Daksha's arrogance.

The Tandava rippled through the fabric of being, each motion a law rewritten in pain and brilliance.

His eyes, once pools of sorrow, became twin conflagrations—unforgiving, merciless, just.

Then came the moment heavy with inevitability—
Shiva no longer stood as the grieving husband but as
Bhairava, the implacable enforcer of dharma.

25

Salutations to the Golden-eyed Lord

Om Piṅgalalochanāya Namaḥ

I stood, unmoving, at the foot of my Lord's dais, the air an ash-strewn altar after the Tandava's final, heart-wrenching beat.

The apocalyptic resonance faded, but the silence that descended was not peace; it was the ominous, predictive hush before a new epoch.

The pantheon of gathered gods stilled, their myriad worlds suspended in their motion, and I understood:

this moment was the sublime unveiling of universal law and the turning of the eternal wheel.

I remain, the unblinking, eternal vehicle of His will, rooted in devotion at the nexus where all creation is undone and begins anew.

Om.

26

I Bow to the Bearer of the Trident

Om Śūlapāṇaye Namaḥ

I witnessed His fierce, luminous form tempering the rigorous fire of justice, His wrath folding back into the deep well of compassion.

He gave the nod of decree, a sanction heavier than the movement of planets.

Life would be returned, but the indelible sin of arrogance would not be erased without a mark.

Daksha's contemptuous human head was gone, consumed and purified by the cleansing fires of the Tandava, vanished as if it had never been.

A symbolic replacement was required, one that would forever bear the physical mark of his lack of his disrespect.

Only the head of the humble male goat—the very creature consecrated for the sacrifice Daksha had stained with his pride—remained worthy.

Such was the Truth: the goat—emblem of selfless sacrifice—would supplant the head that had fostered ego-driven ritualism.

It was the imposition of supreme humility, a horn-crowned vigil against all future vanity.

27

Salutations to the Wielder of the Sword

Om Khaḍgapāṇaye Namaḥ

The judgment of the cosmos softened, revealing once more the Mahadeva—the husband lost in sorrow.

My Lord turned from the ritual ground, and every eye followed Him to where the perfect, lifeless form of Sati lay.

He approached her, His hands, which held the power to dissolve creation, now moved with infinite tenderness.

He lifted the sacred, inert body and placed it upon His shoulder. Thus began the unending procession.

It was not the mourning of a god, but the turning of the universe toward its deepest grief.

Om Namah Shivaya.

28

Salutations to the Divine Bearer of Skulls

Om Kaṅkāline Namaḥ

He did not walk the earth or the mountains; He walked the boundaries of existence.

We followed the Lord — I, the eternal vehicle — across the three worlds, Shiva's lament shaking the very pillars of the cosmos.

His penance was this: to carry the burden of His love, refusing to acknowledge the finality of her death.

He was neither Destroyer nor Creator now, but merely the Great Bearer of unending sorrow.

The movement of the worlds stalled beneath the weight of His grief.

29

Homage to the Ash-Grey Eyed Lord

Om Dhūmralochanāya Namaḥ

I began to behold a truth far more terrifying than wrath: in that sanctified quietude, the loving form of Mahadeva was consumed by the living fate of His own truth.

His grief had forged the diamond blade of justice, and from the chasm of His sorrow rose Bhairava, the embodiment of the terrible, inescapable face of cosmic necessity and inevitable law.

Bhairava's gaze burned cold for within him was a fury where love and wrath merged.

The earth recoiled beneath his roaring heart, as the benevolent Lord became unravelled, unbound, untamed.

From the depths of his third eye's deadly flame, Bhairava was birthed as a raging tempest slicing through pride's false veil.

Silence was shattered by the thunder of his grief for even the cosmos shook at the tremor of his rage.

Bhairava was ordained to champion justice and eradicate deceit.

In Bhairava's scrutiny, the old world found its cage.

30
Salutations to the Fearless One Who Removes All Dread

Om Abhirave Namaḥ

Sati's holy essence,
the scattered dust
that remained
having abandoned
the confines of mortal flesh
was dismembered as
the foundation of
all future reality.

The affliction of Sati's demise had been alchemised; forged into the supreme, immutable instrument of the cosmos.

Her dissolution
the very genesis
of universal life
across the epochs
is a divine
life-giving rain
bearing
the resilient seed of renewal
concealed within
the heart of ruin.

31

Homage to Lord Bhairava, the Supreme Master

Om Bhairavināthāya Namaḥ

While Shiva wandered the cosmos, clutching Sati's body, Vishnu, moved by compassion, deployed his Sudarshana Chakra.

The divine discus cleaved the beloved body of Sati, gentle piece by gentle piece.

I watched, weeping, as the fragments fell like life-giving rain upon the earth.

Where each part touched the ground, it became a sacred nexus, an eternal confluence of Sati's divine energy.

It was in this way that tragedy was transmuted into eternal grace.

32

I Bow to the Protector from Evil Spirits

Om Bhūtapāya Namaḥ

The boundless silence awakened, revealing Mahadeva's form as pure, eternal, infinite, light.

The scattered parts of the Goddess Sati became holy living sites—the Shakti Pithas—where Her power would reside forever.

These places were destined to remain eternally as silent witnesses to Her eternal grace, embodying the

mystery of the transcendence of the Living Truth beyond form and name.

Once the final fragment of the goddess had consecrated the earth, and the divine act of dispersal was complete, my Mahadeva stood empty upon the firmament.

33

Praise to the Lord of the Yoginis

Om Yoginīpataye Namaḥ

The agonising *anava* of separation had been lifted, but in its place settled an austerity so vast it threatened to consume Him whole.

His sorrow transmuted
into the austere determination
that precedes a new age.

I waited, ever ready for His next command.

He uttered no command, yet His intent was clearer than any bellow: retreat.

34

Salutations to the Provider of Wealth

Om Dhanadāya Namaḥ

He turned toward the great northern peaks, toward the untouched, eternal isolation of Mount Kailasa.

He did not walk; He ascended, His spirit soaring ahead of His body.

I followed the Lord, maintaining the respectful distance demanded by such solitude.

The destination was the absolute stillness, the deep, secret space where He would retreat into the purest form of meditation, a *tapas* meant to heal His splintered being.

As He settled upon the highest, most frozen summit, wrapping Himself in the silence of ages, I assumed my unmoving posture at the gate. I became the eternal guardian, the silent sentry, the *vahana* who would not move until commanded.

My purpose was to protect the Lord from all intrusion, but truly, it was to protect the cosmos from the sheer, annihilating force of His concentrated energy.

35

Homage to the Destroyer of Wealth

Om Dhanahāriṇe Namaḥ

When the smoke of Daksha's yajna, the fire sacrifice, had thinned, the Lord withdrew.

The rage that once shook the heavens had fallen silent, and He turned away from all that still breathed.

Toward the northern mountains, the Roof of the World, He retreated—a realm where only silence

could exist, a dwelling place where no heart dared to even remember Her name.

I followed as far as I was allowed.

The Lord's steps left no trace upon the earth for even the snow would not touch His feet.

36

I Bow to the Possessor of Great Riches

Om Dhanavate Namaḥ

The withdrawal of the Lord was the withdrawal of Divine Consciousness itself. The worlds did not cease turning, but they grew colder, less vibrant, shadowed by the absence of Shakti.

The balance was violently disturbed.

There was no longer a Divine Mother to temper the Destroyer, and the universe felt the chilling vacuum of her loss, awaiting the moment of her inevitable return.

Thus I remained, stone-still, my gaze fixed upon the unmoving figure of my Lord.

I am the silence outside the silence, the patience that witnesses the unfolding of cosmic time, awaiting the single word or the single movement that will draw Shiva back from His absolute solitude.

I stand, the Gatekeeper of His sorrow and of His solitude.

37

Salutations to the One Endowed with Brilliance

Om Pratibhanavate Namaḥ

There, in the high Himalayas, He sat in stillness. The wind circled Him, gentle now, as though the mountains themselves bowed in mourning.

His eyes closed once again, not for meditation alone, but for retreat—from all that was, from all once loved and later lost.

I waited at His side, keeping vigil through ages, knowing that from His silence, she would one day rise again—no longer as Sati, but the eternal Shakti, born from His very stillness.

Now, no word passed His lips. His matted hair, heavy with ice, lay over His shoulders. His breath was hardly a breath at all. The gods did not approach; for even they feared the calm that follows divine fury.

Only the wind circled Him, carrying the faint scent of her ashes across the peaks.

38

Hail to the Wearer of Serpents

Om Nāgahārāya Namaḥ

The Himalayas, a womb of stony water and wind, received Him and welcomed him like an old friend. There He sat—crossed-legged upon the cold breast of the world, His eyes closed, His body as still as death, yet I knew the inner fire in him burned.

When silence returned, the Master's sorrow came like a tide. His eyes fell upon the ruins, not in triumph, but with a grief no cosmos could bear. I saw Him turn away from that place, carrying nothing of the world with Him—not even His anger.

He walked north, to where no sound followed, to where solitude itself seemed afraid to approach.

There was a déjà vu to all of this. The inner knowing that we had known each other before and that we would know each other again.

39

Praise to the Master of Serpent Power

Om Nāgakeśāya Namaḥ

At times, it seemed He was not mourning but remembering—each moment of her laughter, each spark of their union, burning in the stillness of His meditation.

Yet the stillness was not peace. It was a vow.

I remained at a distance, guarding that vow.

For I understood He was weaving again what had been torn—the bond of creation itself. From His grief, the worlds would one day be reborn.

Until that dawn, I stood waiting, a disciple at the feet of my Lord, listening to the heartbeat of Kailash through the frozen earth.

Om.

40

Homage to the Lord Whose Hair is the Cosmic Space

Om Vyomakeśāya Namaḥ

The moment my Lord settled upon the highest, most ancient peak, He did not only meditate; He became meditation.

The mountain, the sky, the air—all became a single, seamless garment of absolute stillness.

This silence was the overwhelming presence of *Omkara*, the Primal Vibration—unheard by the ears, yet resounding in the deepest chambers of the soul.

I, Nandi, the eternal vehicle, stood guard at the threshold where the manifested world ends and the unmanifested begins.

I had no duties of protection against external demons or lesser gods. My true service was to uphold the integrity of the Lord's penance against the ceaseless chaos of the cosmos.

The entirety of my inner being was an instrument attuned only to Him.

Om.

41

Homage to the Bearer of the Skull

Om Kapālabhṛte Namaḥ

He neither spoke nor moved, yet the instructions were clearer than any command whispered across the eons.

Through the current of silence, I came to understand the true purpose of his *tapasya* penance.

He was absorbing the deepest pain of the universe, integrating the agony of Sati's loss into the

unshakeable certainty of the knowledge that nothing and no one is ever truly separate.

His sorrow was becoming One with the Universal Consciousness.

My journey as his *vahana* was not one of movement towards the Lord, but one of perfect stillness with the Lord.

In this deep, unmoving watch, I learnt the true definition of devotion.

Time, fear, hope, and memory—all dissolved into the luminous cold. My heart became the silent echo of His silence, beating only to the rhythm of the universal Truth.

I am the Gatekeeper of this Kailasa, the sole witness to the God who, through His total detachment, holds the entirety of attachment.

I remain, listening always, for the beat of the *damaru*. Till then, my task is to guard the vast solitude that is, in truth, the only sanctuary for all creation.

Part 4
Kala

Time

42

I Bow to the Lord of Time

Om Kālaya Namaḥ

Why was this her fate? I have pondered upon this question myself.

He is Shiva, my Lord, My Mahadeva.

She is Shakti, the manifestation of the universe which cannot be contained or constrained by the ego.

Her destiny was to serve as the bridge between two realms: the ordered material world—embodied by Daksha's kingdom of strict rules and hierarchical regiments—and the boundless consciousness that Shiva embodies through his limitless nature.

Sati *chose* the act of severance. She released the identity of the false self—the 'Daksha's daughter' identity—which had become a prison. Her self-immolation was the necessary sacrifice required to birth Bhairava.

Her fate was the force—the Living Truth within—that ignited the inescapable justice that followed.

She was the living nexus where rigid worldly order was released to birth spiritual freedom.

Self-sacrifice was chosen—not to embrace death, but to incinerate the last impurity that binds the finite self.

43

Praise be to the One Adorned with a Garland of Skulls

Om Kapālamāline Namaḥ

Sati's fate,
the suffering she endured,
had not been arbitrary.

It was the gravitational pull necessary
for Shiva to birth Bhairava
the God of Justice.

The pyre had consumed
Sati the woman,

but it had consecrated
Bhairava the Judge.

No ego,
however powerful,
is ever permitted
to violate
the sacred principle
of Divine Union
without facing
the inevitable
dreadful price.

44

Homage to the Exquisitely Beautiful Lord

Om Kamanīyāya Namaḥ

The grave injustice of Daksha's *adharma* sparked the sacrifice of Sati, from whose sacred ashes Bhairava arose as a fiery manifestation of consequence.

Sati's defining act of self-sacrifice birthed Bhairava who was destined to be the Kshetrapala—the guardian god of every sacred site where her body fell.

Shiva's wandering, the Tandava of His sorrow, scattered Sati's fragments across the earthly expanse, creating the sacred geography of the fifty-one Shakti Pithas.

Every fragment of Shakti became a focal point of power and Bhairava became the sentinel guarding each fragment of her Truth.

He watches over the ground where her Truth fell, ensuring that the cosmic balance—bought with her self-sacrifice—remains eternally inviolate.

Bhairava is the embodiment of divine retribution and vigilance, guarding the sanctity consecrated by Sati's dismemberment.

He is the guardian who reminds all creation that the injustice—the denial of the True Self—is always met by the relentless and necessary force of Divine law.

Om Shakti.

45

Salutations to the Lord Who Holds the Phases of the Moon

Om Kalānidhaye Namaḥ

This is the definitive terror of fate: it appears dressed as free will.

Did Sati *choose* the fire? Yes, it may appear to be so. But was she free to choose anything other than the means by which the Truth would be unveiled? I do not believe so.

The shards of her body are now scattered across the land, each a lesson in the Living Truth.

When the Judge Kala Bhairava was born, he was roaring with Shiva's grief, as he bore in his hand the skull of Daksha, the sacred *kapala*.

Bhairava, the Judge, did not arrive to grant her temporary relief. He arrived to establish, for all perpetuity, the eternal consequences of the finality of her decision.

Bhairava was birthed to ensure that the cycle of separation and purification were executed perfectly.

The silence on Kailasa, the grief of my Lord, the guardianship of the Shakti Pithas—are all a testament to the Living Truth: you cannot claim to love the eternal and expect to live by the rules of the transient.

To break the bonds of ego, the bondage of the body must also be broken.

Sati's fate was the definition of her Shakti, realised in the self-sacrifice of the flames of purification, and immortalised in the terrifying vigil of Bhairava.

She chose the inevitable, and in doing so, she became the inevitability.

46

Salutations to the Lord of Past, Present, and Future

Om Trilocanāya Namaḥ

I, Nandi, the eternally watchful Guardian of the Gate, stood upon the mountain's frozen brow and saw the entirety of time laid bare.

Mortals call it 'tragedy' or 'choice,' but the eyes of a true devotee of Shiva see only the turning of the Great Wheel of Time.

Sati's suffering, terrible though it was, was the price of establishing Dharma, the foundation of cosmic

balance. Sati's fate was to be the thread that had to break so the great, dark weaver, Kāla—who is Shiva, who is Bhairava—could re-stitch the cosmos.

The fire born of Sati's self-sacrifice was the inevitable closure of a destined chapter. Even the great gods cannot sidestep the cosmic debt, the precise geometry of their own unfolding.

Bhairava is the eternal truth that destiny is not a river you can circumvent, but the current that defines your shores.

No prayer, no ritual, no flight, no human will could have averted it.

The time for Justice was decreed and Sati's fate was the bell tolling its arrival.

The cycle turned, precisely, eternally.

All we can do is witness the absolute terror and beauty of that necessity.

47

Praise to the One with the Burning Vision

Om Jvalannetrāya Namaḥ

Why, oh why, was this her terrible, final and irreversible fate?

When Daksha's voice,
cold and measured,
spoke the words of rejection,
they did not merely
exclude Shiva.

They sought to define Sati
as nothing more
than a daughter,
than a wife,
than a consort
a possession
whose worth
was dictated
by his approval.

This was the injustice: the denial of her sacred autonomy.

48

Homage to the Wielder of the Trident

Om Triśikhinē Namaḥ

Her destiny was not a passive decree. It was the ferocious necessity of upholding her own reality.

Her severance—the leaping into the pyre—was the greatest act of free will, a choice that shredded the contract of her birth to honour the covenant of her marriage.

She chose to burn the vessel that contained the insult, asserting that her identity belonged only to her own innate sense of sovereignty.

The living flame that claimed her was the explosive consequence of embodying a truth too bright for the mundane world to bear.

49

Praise to the Sovereign of the Triple World

Om Trilōkapāya Namaḥ

Bhairava was birthed from the searing, personal woundedness of loss.

Shiva, the Lord of Detachment, heard the distant whisper of her pain and felt the sudden, terrifying silence where her life had been.

His meditation shattered.

That calm, that icy indifference that Daksha had mocked, was instantly replaced by a grief so absolute it demanded physical form.

This agonising choice echoed across the three worlds, but nowhere did it land with such crushing force as upon the peak of Kailasa.

50

Homage to the Son of the Three-Eyed Lord

Om Trinetraṭanayāya Namaḥ

Baba Bhairava, Father Time, did not arise from detached principle or impersonal justice. He was born from the raw, visceral fracture of woe—a wound so intimate that it catapulted a relentless force of revolution.

Bhairava did not argue Sati's case—he answered it, steel and storm in his hands, severing the proud head that had driven her to the flames.

In that single stroke, the ego that mocked the Goddess was silenced.

Sati's choice stood transfigured—not madness, not weakness, but a Living Truth so potent that even a king's neck had to be severed before it.

Daksha's beheading did not descend from a verdict from a distant court. It tore through the *yajna* with a cry from a heart split open by Sati's living flame.

When Shiva carried her consumed form, scattering the Shakti Pithas in his grief-fuelled Tandava, Bhairava followed.

He became the eternal Kshetrapala, the guardian god of sacred sites and the Justice bought by Sati's suffering. He stands guard eternally to ensure that no creature, human or divine, can ever again commit the core injustice: forcing a living being to deny their own sovereignty.

Bhairava's gaze is the protective armour of a guardian god who knows the price of a grieving heart. His only mandate was to ensure that Sati's self-sacrifice was not in vain.

His presence as a guardian divinity confirms that fate is the agonising, glorious duty to live and die by the Living Truth you dare to claim as your very own.

51

Homage to the Divine Child

Om Ḍimbhāya Namaḥ

Bhairava walks the paths of the world, never resting, never placated.

His appearance of nakedness is the terrifying truth that he is beyond all covering, all pretence, all ritual order.

He carries the *Kapala*, the skull of Daksha, a horrific crown that serves as a symbol of human transience.

The head of ego, when severed, becomes the vessel for self-awareness.

Bhairava, Baba Bhairava, the Divine Father, is the Guardian of Time and the Master of the Cremation Grounds… the liminal place where all illusions are reduced to ash.

Every time a soul chooses integrity over comfort, every time a person burns the lie and claims their painful truth, Bhairava guards the validity of their choice.

He is the boundary. He is the end of the argument. He is the swift, final word spoken for Sati, asserting that the cost of denying love's truth is always, inevitably, everything.

He ensures that the fissure Sati opened in Daksha's world remains as a permanent and necessary opening—a path for those who dare to choose freedom over false allegiance.

52

I Bow Before the Peaceful One

Om Śāntāya Namaḥ

When Daksha spoke, his words were not merely slights.

They were a chisel, trying to carve away Sati's selfhood, claiming she was nothing more than a daughter, a possession whose lineage was now forfeit.

When Sati arrived, the air around her was not welcome, but denial of her true nature.

I saw the glint off Daksha's golden regalia. It was heavier than the insult he carried.

You must look closely at what happened in that hall, for fate is not a predestined decree; it is the consequence of Truth.

53

Praise to the Beloved of Peaceful Beings

Om Śāntajanapriyāya Namaḥ

Daksha, the Prajapati, stood rigid, a flawless monument to his own pride, entirely convinced he was duty-bound to purge his house of her choice.

The hall of Daksha's sacrifice was a furnace of self-righteous judgment, suffocating under the weight of gold and formal cruelty.

Far away on Kailasa, the moment she burned, my Lord felt the precise, physical impact of her shame—the irreparable disgrace that had driven her to such an end.

Sati endured the shame of being made a pariah in the only home she had ever known, and the crushing, public humiliation of her sacred choice.

Thus was born the purpose of Bhairava's perpetual vigil. He stands guard, not against demons, but against the reappearance of prideful judgment.

54

I bow to the Lord of Eternal Youth

Om Baṭukāya Namaḥ

Sati's father, Daksha, had all the money, all the power, all the pride of his lineage.

Instead of *supporting* his daughter, he chose, instead, to diminish and devalue her.

He chose to elevate himself... at her expense. He was willing to sacrifice his daughter's life to protect the fragile illusion of his own absolute control.

Daksha's vast power meant he could have chosen peace. He could have used his influence to say, "My daughter loves Shiva and I accept it."

This benevolent act would have validated Sati and bridged the gap between his ordered world and Shiva's freedom.

But he *refused*.

To support Sati was to acknowledge that the Supreme Being was superior to the ego's carefully guarded rules. It would shatter his false belief that he was the most important being in the cosmos.

Daksha chose separation because agreement meant that he would have to humble himself.

55

I Bow to the One with Diverse Appearances

Om Bahuveśāya Namaḥ

Daksha's error was fuelled by a primordial pride—an ego so vast it eclipsed all wisdom and vehemently separated the divine ties meant to unite.

He was the great administrator, the keeper of sacred laws, the one who decided who was worthy and who was not. His entire world was built on rules, hierarchy, and perfect separation.

My Lord Shiva, however, represents complete unadulterated freedom. He is the true reality—the beggar who needs nothing, the Lord who recognises no rules, thriving even in the chaos of the cremation grounds.

Daksha's downfall was his ego's desperate need to be supreme. His grand sacrifice was not a religious gathering. It was a carefully-staged political attack on Sati. He invited every god and every sage, ensuring the world watched as he intentionally left his own daughter's portion empty.

His message was clear: You, Sati, and your husband, are not important to me. You are *nothing* without me.

By the end, she faced her father, not as a child, but as a sovereign demanding justice.

56

Salutations to the Wielder of the Skull-Topped Staff

Om Khaṭvāṅgavaradhārakāya Namaḥ

He who has the power and the means to bestow grace should not use it to enforce arrogance. The ego mistakes the transient and the temporary for the truth.

By denying Sati's soul purpose—to manifest the Truth of existence—Daksha denied the very essence of life. He burnt his own child to keep the gilded throne from crumbling.

Daksha, cold and cruel, saw only a danger to his authority.

"Your worth is derived from your loyalty to my house and my rules. You abandoned both. Your life is worthless here. You are cast out from my family, my rite, and my protection."

That moment—the realisation that her father preferred his system to her soul—was Sati's fate. The body she wore was a product of Daksha's prideful world.

Her overcoming was the most painful act of self-reliance: she decided the link had to be absolutely broken.

57

I Bow to the Lord Who Governs All Beings

Om Bhūtādhyakṣāya Namaḥ

She turned from her father, her spirit fixed on the truth of Shiva.

"This form, which experienced the ultimate insult, cannot continue!" she cried.

Through the intense power of her *yoga* spiritual focus, she commanded the inner fire of her own being to ignite. She ascended in flames, deliberately

destroying the flesh that tied her to Daksha's flawed lineage.

Sati's sacrifice was the thunderous end of her dependence.

58

Homage to the Master of All Bound Souls

Om Paśupataye Namaḥ

My Lord, the Ash-Smeared Mahadeva, sat immovable—His silence the only sound in the cosmos, for the very axis of existence had shifted.

Sati, the Living Truth, was gone.

Yet, the story does not end here. No, no, it cannot. It merely begins anew once more.

The Divine Spark, Sati's eternal spirit, was re-housed in Parvati, the daughter of Himavan.

The Mountain King—firm, silent, and unshakable— offered her the very foundation Daksha had maliciously refused: unconditional acceptance.

She grew, not burdened by expectation, but fortified by an iron knowledge: the previous life had been lost because her power was tethered to another's affection and approval.

59

Homage to the Mendicant One

Om Bhikṣukāya Namaḥ

By the time Sati reincarnates, she is no longer Sati. She will never be Sati ever again. She will never again be bound by the rituals of her ancestral legacy and lineage.

The protective fury of Bhairava successfully carved out a sacred space, ensuring that when Sati finally returned, reborn as Mother Parvati, the world she entered would be one defined by sovereignty, not lineage.

Bhairava, the keeper of the memory, confirms that the righteous ransom would be paid for the integrity of their love.

The violence done in the hall of Daksha ensured that the next union is one of spiritual equality, free from all hierarchical constraint.

In the fullness of time, driven only by an unspoken summon, she seeks Shiva once again—he, who has waited through the rise and fall of all the ages.

She finds my Lord still locked in deep penance, his heart frozen by the memory of her shame. Bhairava's birth, however, had ensured that the terms have changed.

The fierce Father Guardian Bhairava demands that Shiva recognise Parvati's True Self not through easy inheritance, but by the virtue of the rigorous, self-chosen devotion *tapasya* she undertakes.

160

In the womb of that terrifying protection, the perfect story begins.

Om Shakti.

60

I bow to the Lord in the Guise of a Servant

Om Paricārakāya Namaḥ

Her rebirth as Parvati, the daughter of the Mountain King Himavan was the beginning of true strength.

Her new father gave her the unconditional support of stability. She was born of the stable, enduring mountain earth, free from the vanity of illusionary courtly titles.

Parvati was destined to undertake decades of gruelling penance *tapasya*. This was her journey of restoration and recovery: rebuilding her identity, not seeking her father's approval, but proving her power to herself.

She showed the universe that her devotion was the unshakeable, supreme power—forged in solitude and independent of any external source.

She returned to Shiva as his equal, the embodiment of an enduring love that triumphs over the separation chosen by her former father.

61

Homage to the One Who Outwits the Forces of Illusion

Om Dhūrtāya Namaḥ

Parvati already knew of the grave error: to approach the Great Yogi as Sati's grieving memory would be weakness, a plea for external validation.

Thus began the great undoing. She walked away from the mountain palace, shedding the silk of dependency and the softness of comfort.

Her penance, her *tapasya*, changed from a ritual of piety to a conscious and deliberate act of self-creation.

She was no longer Sati and would never be Sati ever again.

Her mission was to cease seeking Shiva and, instead, become the fundamental, inescapable force that would draw Him from His trance.

The *anava* of separation between Shiva and Shakti was destined to be dissolved.

Part 5
Tapasya

Purification

62

I Bow to the One whose Garment is Space

Om Digambarāya Namaḥ

Behold the Lady of the Mountain, standing utterly alone! *Parvati Mahadevaya!*

When the Himalayan winter howled, she stood as a living icicle, letting the glacial winds scour her skin, burning away every remnant of insecurity.

She undertook the trial of the five fires, where the spirit is tempered through heat, like metal seeking its

purest form. It was here, in this divine furnace, that she forged the core of her being.

She burned away the lingering desire for approval, the systematic rejection of Daksha, and the very need for Shiva's external glance.

In her state of surrender, she shattered every chain of dependence, becoming a flame of pure freedom — where nothing remained but the infinite self, luminous, radiant and unbound.

When the vicious summer arrived, she stood amidst the five sacred fires. Four flames surrounded her as the fifth, the merciless sun, shone above.

Her self-sacrifice was not a loss, but a liberation, a sacred severance that opened the soul to its own eternal light.

Om.

63

Homage to the Hero of Heroes

Om Śauriṇe Namaḥ

I come to You, compassionate Lord, with a humble heart. Teach me to see karma with Your eyes—not as fate, but as a deep, Living Truth flowing through all existence, a path where Your hand guides the unseen causes and effects.

Help me understand, soothe my restless spirit, so I may move through joy and suffering alike, held within Your unending love and the silent justice of Your will.

Two farmers toil side by side upon the earth, one reaps a bountiful harvest, while the other returns empty-handed, though their hands and efforts were the same, their fruits diverge—is it karma, O Shiva, that whispers this secret, for unseen consequences weave the unfolding of fruit from seed?

O Great Lord Shiva, whose grace touches all beings, though all souls bear within them the command to experience karma, I see some rise in heavenly joy while others suffer in pain… How is it that such differing fates unfold from the same cosmic dance?

64

I bow to the Controller of the Restless Mind

Om Hariṇāya Namaḥ

O Supreme Being, O Supreme Soul, O Mahadeva, Your will moves with the vastness of a wisdom which can neither be bent nor broken.

Through the gaze of your boundless and limitless mercy, You bless your devotees to see beyond the lingering shadows of karma.

To those souls who carry only the last trace of impurity—the veil of *anava mala*—You offer grace, tender and precise.

To every seeker whose heart aches for the Living Truth, to the great souls who embody infinite being—Your mercy flows according to the journey of each soul's unfolding. Each at a unique place in the unfolding of *anava mala*'s ripening.

Your grace ascends gently, Lord,
bound not by the weight of past deeds.

It flows freely from
Your endless compassion,
guiding each soul
with subtle wisdom
toward the light.

In this surrender, I find peace—knowing it is Your will alone that leads me home, not the chains of karma, but Your loving hand that steers me softly in this sacred unfolding

O Mahadeva, in Your presence, all burdens dissolve. Teach me to trust in Your boundless grace, to rest in the quiet knowing that Your will never errs—for Your love carries me beyond all shadows into the chandelier of infinite light.

65

I Bow to the Lord of Clear Vision

Om Pāṇḍulocanāya Namaḥ

O Shiva, I know there is no cruelty in Your choices. Cruelty wounds and confines, but Your will is the unfolding of lasting peace and joy—pure happiness that outshines all suffering.

On this sacred path, the sweetness of joy endures as a quiet light in the heart, eternal, luminous and free.

In the hearts of those walking the pure path, the shadows within—the primordial impurity called

anava mala—softens and matures through the temperate timing of Your unseen grace.

When the inner ripeness has been reached, You alone place each soul in its rightful place in time, granting varied joys, not by the harsh hand of karma, but by Your boundless compassion.

Let me surrender to Your wise and loving guidance, accepting that Your design is not merely bound by merit or fate, but by the divinity of Your compassion that leads every soul gently home.

Through Your grace, my spirit find rests and rises anew.

66

I Bow to the Eternally Tranquil Lord

Om Praśāntāya Namaḥ

O Lord Paramesvara, whose presence is the axis of all worlds, I come to You with the weight of my many questions and the silences repeatedly born and reborn of my doubts.

What are these karmas? Are they the restless waves of *prakruti* that swirl without purpose? Are they qualities tied to the soul itself—an intimate thread we carry within?

My heart, overwhelmed by voices and uncertainties, turns to You alone. Reveal to me, O Mahadeva, the true nature and purpose of karma, not as mere law or punishment, but as the sacred rhythm woven by Your will.

Through Your compassion, make clear what hides in shadow. Let Your light be the infinite flame that destroys the darkness.

I surrender this seeking to You, the eternal Lord, knowing that You alone are the source from which the Living Truth flows unbroken.

67

Homage to the Granter of Tranquillity

Om Śāntidāya Namaḥ

O Lord Shiva, Supreme Being and eternal witness, I bring before You the tangled threads that puzzle my heart.

This *prakruti*, the ever-changing world around us cannot be the cause—for how can that which is itself the object of enjoyment give rise to that joy?

If *prakruti,* the primal nature, is but a field where the soul's play unfolds, then karma must be something other, something subtle and deep.

Karma flows from the shifting dispositions of our intellect, the eight *pratyayas,* the eight mental dispositions… These are not merely thoughts, but the hidden patterns which shape how we see and respond, the silent currents that colour our experience and guide karma's flow along their predestined path.

Each soul carries its own unique arrangement of these inner tendencies and this unevenness reveals that they must spring from something beyond themselves. For how could these subtle patterns create their own difference without another cause?

But even those vary from soul to soul, uneven as the ripples churning within a restless sea. How can such diversity arise from itself alone? What cause lies beyond, to weave this manifold dance of being?

This leads me beyond reason, beyond the endless cycles of cause and effect, into the embrace of Your infinite will—where all contradictions dissolve and the mystery of diversity and unity is held tenderly in Your cosmic heart.

Help me dissolve the endless circle that traps thought and guide me to see the truth beyond reason, where your boundless will crafts the mystery of diversity and unity, holding all souls within your infinite embrace.

68

Homage to the Ultimate Master

Om Siddhāya Namaḥ

The dispositions of the mind—the *pratyayas*—appear even in those who have turned away from worldly actions, still in silence and restraint.

How then, O Lord, could these quiet stirrings be the root cause of the vast, shifting forms of the world—matter's manifold play?

The soul's journey outward—engaging with the world, seeking, grasping, living in the flow of action and desire. It is the movement toward life's experiences, the pulse of involvement in the dance of existence.

The soul's journey inward—the gentle retreat from worldly ties, the quiet letting go, where the soul turns toward stillness and surrender, resting in the embrace of Your infinite silence.

These two are like the tide's coming and going, opposite yet part of the same eternal ocean, where the soul learns both to hold and to release.

Help me, O Compassionate One, to find balance between these currents, to act without attachment and rest without fear and to walk this path towards You with steady heart and open eyes, held together by Your boundless grace.

For in the same heart, birth and cessation, movement and stillness, exist as opposite truths both born from an unchanging essence.

O Shiva, reveal to me, how the eternal can hold, within itself, such seeming contradiction and the silent source from which all dualities bloom; beyond infinite regress, beyond self-caused cycles…

Guide me into the embrace of Shiva's great mystery, where all truths dance in loving unity, held by Your boundless grace.

69

I bow to the Beloved Kinsman of Śaṅkara

Om Śaṅkarapriyabandhavāya Namaḥ

In the quiet chambers of my mind, I seek to grasp the truth of these *pratyayas* mental dispositions— the eight subtle ways knowledge moves within us. They are not separate lights, but countless shades of one great awareness, shifting gently like colours emerging upon the rainbow.

Sattva is the stillness that sees with clarity, receiving the world exactly as it flows—unchanged, unbiased, whole. *Rajas* is the impatient flame that stirs the

waters, weaving movement and desire into the fabric of life. *Tamas* is the heavy shadow, the darkness of untruth that hinders knowing as it waits for the dawn.

True ignorance, beloved Lord, lies deeper still—born not of tamas, but from the primal *mala*, the thick veil that Your grace alone can lift.

Open my heart to this subtle truth, where light and shadow are not enemies, but dancers in Your boundless play which lead me beyond the obscuration to rest quietly in Your eternal love.

70

Salutations to the Lord of Eight Forms

Om Aṣṭamūrtaye Namaḥ

O Lord Shiva, in the sacred silence, in the elusive moments where the mind turns entirely towards You, I finally unravelled the hidden force of karma. Where one fruit unfolds in time, while another, ripe and potent, waits in the shadows.

If this new fruit bears greater weight, it can quiet the one now ripening, like a stronger wave smoothing the fleeting ripple beneath. They mingle and weave

through the same field of existence—a tapestry of interconnected lives, shifting in forms both subtle and raw.

When fate lingers on the fragile edge and the karmic fruit that is destined calls louder—Your will, O Mahadeva, unfolds the great mystery, dissolving one life to birth another or merging both where destiny permits.

When two equal and opposing karmas meet, in that moment, Your gentle descent falls like the promise of long overdue rain, dissolving conflict and granting peace beyond all words.

Teach me to trust this vast, unseen design. Permit me to rest in Your ever-present gaze… Where even the shifting winds of karma find stillness in Your grace.

71

Homage to the Master of All Wealth

Om Nidhīśāya Namaḥ

The souls bound by fetters of *mala* wear their chains with silent sorrow.

There are three distinct states veiled by bondage, but only the *sakala* soul bears the weight of all three bonds in its struggle to reclaim the light of the True Self beyond name and form.

The first is *anava mala*, the deepest veil, the seed of ego and separation, the sense that the soul is limited, alone and disconnected from Your infinite Self.

The second is *karma mala*, the binding web of deeds and their fruits, which weaves the soul's path through countless lifetimes, keeping it tethered to the cycle of birth and death, pleasure and pain.

The third is *maya mala*, the shroud of illusion, which blurs true knowing and presents the world as solid and separate, trapping the soul in shadows of misunderstanding and desire.

Bound by these three, the soul moves as if in chains, its knowing dimmed and its power curtailed by these intertwined forces.

Yet, from deep within, a quiet yearning stirs, a call to self-illuminate from this grip and to glimpse the radiant freedom that shines beyond all fetters.

72

Praise to the One with the Vision of Wisdom

Om Jñānacakṣuṣe Namaḥ

The *pralayakala* soul is in a state of partial release. These souls have succeeded in casting off all bonds save for the single, enduring impurity of *karma mala*.

Consequently, their existence is suspended in an intermediate realm between cycles of creation. They are held in this cosmic waiting until the entirety of their past actions is fully exhausted. Only then, with the residue of karma finally dissipated, are they

released to merge into the pure, essential current of the universe.

Deeper still lies the state of the *vijñānākala* soul. This soul confronts only the subtlest burden: *aṇava mala*. This is the core impurity, manifesting as the final, persistent sense of 'I'—the separateness from 'You.' Under the pressure of this primordial ego, the soul's inherent divine powers—pure knowledge *vijñāna* and action *kriyā*—are held in suspension.

Nevertheless, even within this state of darkness, an incandescent spiritual ember remains. This deep and relentless yearning reaches solely for Your boundless grace, for it is this desire that ignites the fire.

This is the fire that burns away all remaining veils to finally unveil the soul's luminous light.

73

I Bow to the Lord Whose Form is Penance

Om Tapomayāya Namaḥ

When Your sacred Shakti descends, it acts with decisive power. Her energy severs the deep potency of mala—the primordial impurity which keeps the soul trapped in the endless cycle of *māyā* illusion and *karma* birth, death and rebirth.

The purification is achieved when all the soul's accrued karmas—marked equally by light and shadow—find themselves in a state of perfect

balance. At this precise moment, Your sacred energy, Śivaśakti, purifies those karmas completely, leaving no imprint or residue behind.

No fruit remains to be born from any action, and the wheel of karmic consequence is decisively stilled.

With the soul thus purified of karma, it attains the state of *vijñānakevala*. This is a pure and luminous existence where the soul stands almost free, burdened only by the subtle residue of *aṇava mala*— the final impurity that marks the last trace of ego.

A silent fire of longing then comes to illuminate the heart: "When shall I see You, Lord? When shall I be free from all chains? Who is the guide, the preceptor, that can lead me to Your Cosmic Abode?"

Some call this liberation, but I know it as the soul resting in the quiet clarity of Your unyielding presence; for when the self's veils are lifted, only Your infinite reality shines.

74

Homage to the Eight Cosmic Aspects

Om Aṣṭādhārāya Namaḥ

O Compassionate One, may Your presence break these shadows wide open and awaken every soul to its radiant truth.

O Compassionate Shiva, look upon these souls with eyes of gentle fire and guide them with Your boundless mercy through the labyrinth of illusion.

May all souls live free within Your eternal embrace and may darkness dissolve and only love remain.

Draw them towards the light of liberation and eternal union with You where chains fall away and only blissful freedom remains.

75

Homage to the Bearer of Six Supports

Om Ṣaḍādhārāya Namaḥ

This awakening is the soul's first breath of true yearning and a sacred unrest that draws it ever closer to Your infinite grace and mercy.

From endless wandering emerges
the eternal embrace of liberation.

With this irreversible severance, the soul is unshackled from its bondage. An unmistakable detachment dawns—a gradual ceasing from the

transient pleasures of the world and the endlessness
of the weary journey through suffering.

O Compassionate One, let me be among those who
awaken,
Who shed all fetters through Your divine touch,
To dwell forever in the shelter of Your boundless
love.

O Merciful One, teach me to walk toward this truth
To surrender into the perfect stillness of Your grace,
Where bondage ends and freedom is born anew.

76

I Bow to the Wielder of Primal Energy

Om Sarpayuktāya Namaḥ

O Lord Shiva, my soul, though bound by *mala*, longs for the vastness of Your truth. How can the spark of wandering desires arise if not for the veil that narrows my vision? Yet beyond this obscuration, Your essence shines pure and limitless.

May my words be vessels, not of empty phrases, but carriers of the quiet weight and delicate yearning within.

Within me is the restless pining of a soul seeking the silent grace of Your lotus feet.

In this sacred space of stillness, let each line unfold like a breath taken deep, awakening the dialogue between the mundane and the infinite—so that poetry becomes a prayer, a meditation and a bridge to the heart of the divine.

May this spirit guide every verse I write, grounded in nature, symbol, and truth, reflecting the sacred journey from shadow into light, where the soul, unbound and free, rests in Your eternal embrace.

77

Salutations to the Friend of the Peacock

Om Śikhīsakhye Namaḥ

O Lord Shiva, in the realm of divine truth, karma exists as twofold—merit and demerit—nestled deeply in the *buddhi tattva*, the seat of discernment. Yet, how can these subtle tapestries of action bind the soul that dwells in the higher planes beyond *buddhi* the intellect?

The soul's limited and conditioned consciousness reflects on experiences as it analyses and forms judgments. It is the mental faculty that enables

reasoning and awareness, shaping how the soul interacts with the world, particularly in evaluating and responding to karmic influences.

Karma governs our deeds and their fruits, the pleasures and pains that weave life's tapestry, but it does not cloak the soul's pure consciousness—the radiant eternity—that shines beyond all veils.

If karma were the source that obscures the soul's luminous essence, it would unravel the ordered harmony of *tattvas*, multiplying endlessly with each new influence, fracturing the delicate balance of cosmic truth.

No, it is not karma mala, but anava mala—an impurity hidden deep within—that veils and confines the divine spark within.

78

Salutations to the Bearer of the Earth

Om Bhūdhārāya Namaḥ

O Lord Shiva, it is known that *mala*, the impurity shrouding the soul, manifests in seven forms—delusion, pride, attachment, sorrow, pain, thirst and confusion.

Moha delusion clouds the mind, obscuring the truth of the divine.

Delusion *moha* is born with the soul; it is without beginning and is the root from which all other six impurities emerge. This primal impurity causes even the wise to falter and desire worldly pleasures. It clouds the heart with illusions about the material world, blurring the line between what should be sought and what should be renounced.

Pride inflates the ego, hiding the soul's infinite humility.

Attachment binds the heart to worldly pleasures, diverting it from the eternal.

Disillusion causes despair and discontent, tearing at the soul's serenity.

Burning pain keeps the soul in perpetual suffering and longing.

Thirst dries the spirit, removing the moisture of divine bliss.

Confusion creates the illusion of separateness, making the One appear many.

May Your grace free me from these seven veils!

Remove the primal delusion that binds my soul and lead me to rest peacefully at Your feet, where truth shines pure and eternal.

79

I Bow to the Supreme Master Who Supports the World

Om Bhūdharādhīśāya Namaḥ

This veil, the *mala*, the impurity, does not extinguish the light. It arrests the soul's power to fully know and do. Like a flame held by a sacred mantra, still glowing but prevented from burning, the soul exists, its knowing and doing slowed, held back.

Though not truly obscured, the soul's activity seems as though it is held in a silence that feels like shadow. Bound closely to this veil, the soul suffers the

condition called *pasutva*, a state of captivity where the soul is veiled from its radiant freedom.

This veil, the *mala* impurity, does not destroy the soul's light but obscures it—blocking the full knowing and doing that is the soul's true state.

Because of this heavy attachment to *mala*, the soul is seen as bound, weighed down by impurity, existing in the state called *pasutva*, the condition of being tethered and limited, like one caught in chains.

80

Homage to the Lord of the Earth

Om Bhūpataye Namaḥ

O Compassionate Shiva,
Teach me to see beyond
The shifting shadows of action and consequence,
To recognise the eternal light within myself,
To seek refuge in Your boundless mercy,
Where the soul transcends veils
and returns to its true
unconditioned home.

81

Homage to the Son of the Mountain Lord

Om Bhūdharātmajāya Namaḥ

O Compassionate Lord,
grant me the strength
To feel beneath
these veils
the constant
Unbroken radiance of my True Self
To awaken and cast off this darkness
and rest forever in the freedom of
Your eternal light and love.

82

Homage to the Bearer of Bones

Om Kaṅkāladhāriṇe Namaḥ

It was through this solitary crucible within that Mother Parvati, Sovereign Mother of the Universe, achieved *Svatantrya*, the supreme, independent will.

She proved, through sheer, unyielding endurance, that her devotion was a self-generated, absolute energy, sufficient unto itself.

She rebuilt her identity from the very dust of the earth, asserting that she, the primordial Shakti, was not a consort waiting to be chosen, but the sovereign power required to awaken and energise the cold, still universe.

Parvati Mahadevaya!

83

I Bow to the Lord of the Skull

Om Muṇḍine Namaḥ

The *tapasya* was the conscious surgery of the self. She abandoned the palace and the mountain's shelter, deliberately entering environments where Her beauty, Her wealth and Her high birth were rendered meaningless.

She submitted to the icy scythe of the Himalayan winter, where her flesh was reduced to the bare truth of bone and spirit. The cold stripped away all vanity and the last, lingering need for external validation and approval.

The *Pancha Agni*, the ordeal of the five fires, was the intense, psychological trial. The scorching heat, day after day, burnt away every remaining impurity forged by society: the desire for an easy path, the expectation of being chosen, and the toxic residue of Daksha's systemic rejection.

She burned her history. She incinerated her dependency. She became an entity whose value was self-created, measured only by her vigil known to none but Shiva.

84

Homage to the Lord Whose Sacred Thread is a Snake

Om Nāgāyajñopavitakāya Namaḥ

She ceased to be the daughter of Himavan, the past life echo of Sati or the seeker of Shiva. She existed purely as the Self-Generated Power *Shakti*.

She was ready to approach the Lord, not as a shadow seeking the light, but as the fully realised Divine Mother, complete in herself, prepared to restore the universe to its perfect, energetic balance.

Only when she had fully transcended the need for the world's recognition—when her inner realisation was so complete that Shiva's acceptance was a cosmic formality—was she ready.

She proved that the individual, when stripped bare of all inherited titles and social context, is not 'nothing,' but everything.

In the vastness of her solitude, Parvati achieved *svatantrya*, the supreme, independent will. She performed the complete act of individual assertion.

Her devotion was no longer an emotional offering. It was a force of nature, forged through absolute, sheer, lonely labour. She built her identity from the very ground up, asserting that she was not a consort waiting for a name, but the Shakti required to revitalise the still, cold universe.

85

Hail to the Lord of Stupor and Inaction

Om Jṛmbhaṇāya Namaḥ

It was only after this immense, resolute, and beautiful labour—having completely transcended the need for the Mountain King's comfort or even Shiva's immediate notice—that she was truly ready.

She approached the grieving, inward-facing Yogi as the fully self-realised, self-created Divine Mother.

Complete in her own right, she stood prepared to restore the Lord to the world and to re-establish the cosmic order and the eternal balance.

The universe held its breath, waiting for the Divine Mother to speak.

86

Homage to the Lord Who Confounds and Charms

Om Mohanāya Namaḥ

She stood before the Great Yogi. He was encased in ice and silence, a beautiful, devastating monument to grief. The world expected her to weep, to plead, to remind him of Sati. She did none of these things. Her presence was an unassailable declaration: I am here. I am complete.

Shiva stirred, not in recognition, but in test.

A subtle smile touched His lips as He projected the illusion of a sceptical wanderer, a voice of reason attempting to dismantle Her devotion.

"Daughter of the Mountain, why do you waste your prime pursuing me? I am the Ash-Smeared, dwelling in cremation grounds. I have no wealth, no home, and no name recognised by the world. You are High Born, bound to a glorious lineage. Go, find a consort worthy of your title, your beauty, and your father's renown."

87

Homage to the One Who Immobilises

Om Stambhinē Namaḥ

It was the trial attempting, once again, to reduce Her to Her external relationships—Daughter, Wife, Mother.

Parvati looked upon Him and her gaze held the stillness of the Himalayas and the heat of the five fires. The test could not touch Her, for the one who speaks of lineage had no power over the one who had burned their lineage to ash.

"You speak of names and titles, but I have paid the price to understand their true emptiness," she replied, her voice resounding with the certainty of absolute truth.

"Your life of austerity is a rejection of the world's false values. My *tapasya* was the equal rejection of the world's false definitions of self."

88

Salutations to the Destroyer of Ignorance

Om Māraṇāya Namaḥ

"I did not come to you seeking a husband to bestow a name upon me," she stated. "I came because I have become the answer to the cosmic imbalance. You are the perfect stillness, the eternal consciousness that rests.

"But the universe demands movement. It demands the flow of action, the current of energy."

She took one final, sovereign step forward. "I have achieved my identity alone. I require no external validation. Now, I simply claim my necessity. I am the manifestation that must animate Your Consciousness.

"The silence must now be complemented by the rhythmic flow of creation."

89

Salutations to the Agitator and Disturber

Om Kṣobhanāya Namaḥ

In that infinitesimal gap between Her command and His acceptance, the cosmos held its breath.

The stars paused. I stood there silently as I always had, a smile emerging across my lips.

Thousands of years of sorrow, held captive within His meditative state, began its slow, agonising retreat. His attention shifted—not outward, but

intensely inward, where the universe inside His consciousness witnessed the truth of her *svatantrya*.

He saw neither the mountain girl, nor the former wife, but the complete freedom that mirrored His own detachment—the only power capable of meeting His solitude without demanding dependency.

This new union was a repudiation of Daksha's world. It proved that Shakti, the individual will, forged through suffering and self-discovery, is not subordinate to Daksha's lineage or her status as Himavan's daughter.

Rather, she stands sovereign and strong as the essential, animating force of Shiva consciousness.

Part 6
Sovereignty

Svatantrya

90

Praise to the Pure and Immaculate one

Om Śuddhāya Namaḥ

A resonant crack echoed across the peaks. The ancient, glacial ice that had encased His form, the visible manifestation of His grief, began to splinter, separating from His divine skin in slow, agonising shards.

Then, the Hair: His matted locks, repositories of the wild, unkempt sorrow, began a majestic unfurling as the thawing rivers were released from a millennia-long winter spell.

They did not fall; they flowed, cascading down His back, signalling the return of the life force.

Finally, the heat: the self-forged golden current of Her energy, forged in the *Pancha Agni*, pulsed forward as an undeniable, irresistible wave. It did not rush; it seeped into Him, melting the very core of ancient sorrow.

91

Homage to the One of Black-Blue Brilliance

Om Nīlāñjanaprakhyāya Namaḥ

When Shiva opened His eyes, they were not the eyes of a Yogi roused from his meditation, but the eyes of the universe viewing its own complete reflection. He saw the entirety of His power, mirrored and affirmed by an equal sovereign.

The individual's radical assertion—that self-creation transcends all lineage—had completed the Divine Union. The distance closed in inevitability.

They merged, forming the *Ardhanarishvara*, the perfect symbol of balance, where the individual will and universal consciousness became one, inseparable truth.

92

Hail to the Destroyer of Demons

Om Daityaghne Namaḥ

Millennia upon millennia of sorrow and grief evaporated in a single blink. He did not extend a hand; He simply allowed the inevitable.

The distance closed. The self-made light of Parvati met the absolute consciousness of Shiva.

The resultant form was the *Ardhanarishvara*, a perfect composite: half pure consciousness, half dynamic power.

It was the physical embodiment that the great, universal being is incomplete without the fully realised, sovereign individual.

93

Homage to the One Adorned by Skulls

Om Muṇḍabhūṣitāya Namaḥ

The cold, still universe had been set in motion, not bound by fate or duty, but by a sovereign who chose to create her own identity and claim her independence.

In that moment, the individual meant everything— the Divine Union where all states of separation are destroyed and dissolved.

The light pulsed once, a singular, complete entity where the gold of Her self-endurance met the ash-white of His eternal detachment.

The form was a living lesson: that spiritual truth is not found in separation, but in balanced union, achieved only when two halves stand in absolute sovereignty.

94

Homage to the Consumer of Sacrificial Offerings

Om Balibhuje Namaḥ

The Himalayas thrummed with a resonance previously unheard.

The Ganges, released from Shiva's locks, surged with renewed vitality.

The three worlds, which had been suffering under the shadow of Shiva's grief-induced inertia, now experienced a wave of perfect cosmic peace.

From the highest heavens, the gods appeared, showering the merged form with flowers of renewal.

They understood that the crisis of separation was over and the universe's work could now resume.

95

Salutations to the Master of Sacrificial Offerings

Om Balibhūnnāthāya Namaḥ

The Divine Union of Shiva and Shakti was the necessary beginning of the universe's work.

The purpose of Parvati's self-creation, her *tapasya*, had not just healed her prior incarnation as the Divine Consort. She had become the sovereign energy required for creation's defence.

Kailasa was transformed. It became the eternal seat of balanced power, a mountain home where the

austerity of Shiva's asceticism and the worldly presence of Shakti united in perpetual harmony.

Parvati, having burned away every trace of lineage and dependency, stood forever as the animating foundation of the Lord, proving to all the worlds that the highest fate is not inherited, but forged, and the true lineage is the one a soul creates for itself.

96

Homage to the Divine Child

Om Bālaya Namaḥ

The Divine Mother does not exist merely to mirror Shiva's glory. She stands as the eternal imperative for action, the constant reminder that consciousness must change.

Her story is a sacred blueprint for every being who feels small against the scale of the cosmos, providing an everlasting answer to the fear that the individual means nothing.

She is the proof that the individual, through self-creation, can become the fundamental necessity of the universe itself.

Parvati's *tapasya* is never finished for it is the unending work of maintaining the balance, the sustained effort of ensuring that the world's false idols of lineage and status never again overshadow the sovereign light of the soul.

97

Homage to the Lord with the Prowess of a Child

Om Bālapārākrāmāya Namaḥ

Now, upon the snow-capped peak of Kailasa, the cosmic drama continues only in the gentle rotation of the stars.

The Great Dance has settled into a balanced stillness. Shiva sits in meditation, His attention vast and silent. Parvati sits beside Him, her gaze open, her energy subtly regulating every vibration of the cosmos.

Their dialogue is no longer spoken but felt—the eternal, silent conversation between Being and Becoming.

In that sacred place, there is no history, no lineage, and no role.

There is only the continuous, perfect state of being fully Self, two sovereign entities eternally unified, demonstrating that completion is found not in the acquisition of titles, but in the hard-won courage to forge forward on the path of one's own truth.

That is the highest, most lasting continuation of the Divine Story.

98

Homage to the Remover of All Obstacles

Om Sarvāpattāraṇāya Namaḥ

Kailasa is the centre point from which *Mahakala* Great Time is judged.

Shiva, the Destroyer, presides over the dissolution of all things, but the presence of Parvati—the self-created power that demands life—ensures that every destruction carries within it the seed of renewal.

Their Divine Union refuses finality—where lineage ends, where external systems break down, where

time seeks to consume all effort and identity, the independence forged by the Divine Mother stands as a counter-force.

It is the eternal, silent promise that the effort of the self is never lost, but woven permanently into the fabric of reality, sustaining the very cycles of cosmic existence.

Thus, the greatest continuation of their story is the existence of the universe itself, vibrating with the courage of her original, solitary assertion.

99

Salutations to the Impregnable Fortress

Om Durgāya Namaḥ

The story is not over, for it is woven into the human heart.

Every time a soul chooses hard-won authenticity over inherited comfort; every time an individual asserts an identity independent of the expectations of their family or society; every time a person finds power in the quiet heat of their own focused will— that is the continuation of Parvati's *tapasya*.

The Divine Mother remains the eternal proof that a single, solitary being, once stripped of all external claim, is not reduced to nothingness, but expands to become the absolute necessity, the indispensable axis around which the world turns.

This is the truth of Kailasa: a sanctuary built upon the unshakeable foundation of the Self, holding the universe in perfect, self-made balance.

100

Homage to the Master of Demonic Entities

Om Duṣṭabhūtaniṣevitāya Namaḥ

On Kailasa, the dust of Sati's humiliation, the long, slow, arduous effort of Parvati's *tapasya*, the crisis of the deities, and the threat of the demonic forces are all reconciled and held in a state of continuous equilibrium.

There is no 'ever after'. There is only the Perpetual Now.

This is the final Living Truth: the story of the self, once fully realised, ceases to be a sequence of events.

It becomes the bedrock of reality itself, a single, unmoving, and eternally self-renewing fact.

In that truth, she remains as the proof that the individual, fully forged, is indistinguishable from the whole.

The light of her self-sovereignty is the continuous dawn that illuminates the Living Truth of existence.

101

Salutations to the Lord Who is Desired

Om Kāminē Namaḥ

Kailasa is the final, perfected canvas of her work. Its very atmosphere is a constant, subtle reminder of the law forged in the inner fire of the flame.

The only hierarchy that matters is the purity of the will.

Upon the peak, every stone, every freezing breath of wind, every droplet from the Ganges acts as a sacred teaching of dharma.

The entrance into this divine domain is granted neither by birthright nor by ritual.

It is earned solely through the solitary perfection of the self.

This final, unmoving truth, imprinted upon the eternal mountain, is the last continuation of Her story: a timeless, physical monument to the soul's triumph over the empty obsessions of lineage and legacy.

102

Homage to the Storehouse of All Skills

Om Kalānidhaye Namaḥ

From that eternal mountain, the unified light of *Ardhanarishvara* radiates eternally.

When the deities, or even the humblest devotee, performs *darshan*, they do not merely *see* Shiva and Parvati; they witness the Universal Law made manifest.

The right side, smeared in ash and silent in meditation, assures them that detachment is the

prerequisite of knowledge. The left side, golden and dynamic, assures them that action is the necessary function of knowledge.

This vision serves as the cosmic judgment: all requests, all prayers, all claims of status are filtered through the lens of her sovereignty.

If the heart seeking an audience is still attached to the ephemeral titles of the world, it trembles before her fierce, self-earned truth.

But if the heart is pure, if the self has been truly found, it finds unconditional acceptance in the unified light, completing the cycle of Her triumph and cementing Her legacy as the Divine Mother of Independent Will.

103
Praise to the Beloved One

Om Kāntāya Namaḥ

Mother Parvati's conquest marks the end of all seeking. She sought Shiva only until She realised she was the necessary complement to Him—that she was the sought.

Thus, the story dissolves the concept of 'the journey' itself.

There is no destination outside the self and no power to be gained from external sources.

Their merged form upon Kailasa is the absolute finality: the seeker and the sought, the student and the knowledge, the individual and the cosmos, are revealed to be eternally one.

All pilgrimage ceases at the base of that mountain, for the truth it embodies is that the power and the purity required for Divine Union reside—and always have resided—within the singular, courageous, self-created heart.

Part 7
The Guardian

Kshetrapala

104

Salutations to the Master Who Subdues Desire

Om Kāminīvaśakṛdvāśinē Namaḥ

I knew, however, that the perfect stillness achieved on Kailasa was a fragile jewel, constantly besieged by the encroaching shadows of cosmic imbalance.

The Divine Couple—now eternally balanced—required an agent of absolute, unyielding enforcement; a terrifying truth whose very existence upheld the peace won by Parvati's solitary fire.

This necessity would manifest, time and again, as Bhairava, the Terrifying, the Fearsome.

He is the thunderous counterpart to the Ash-Smeared Yogi, the active rejection of disorder, the manifestation of Shiva as the Divine Father who establishes and defends the boundaries of reality.

Where Shiva embraced detachment, Bhairava embraced the fight. Where Parvati championed self-sovereignty, Bhairava championed the relentless execution of cosmic law.

Bhairava's task was to prove, through action, the worthlessness of external authority and lineage when pitted against the Living Truth.

105

Homage to the Granter of All Perfect Powers

Om Sarvasiddhipradāya Namaḥ

It was not a demon that forecasted the next birth of the Divine Father of Time. It was the resurgence of *anava mala*—that subtle veil of limitation which dares to eclipse the infinite.

Father Brahma, in his boundless creative fervour, had become convinced of his own singular primacy, mistaking his function for the absolute essence.

This hubris—this clinging to the title of 'Creator' as the ultimate lineage—was the very disease Sati had purged from the cosmos through her self-sacrifice.

If the divine order was to persist, this arrogance, which elevated temporary titles above the Living Truth, had to be violently corrected.

From the burning core of Mahadeva's wrath—a rage born of the necessity to protect the fragile order Parvati had restored—Bhairava was born again.

Bhairava's force arose to confront a deep transgression—Father Brahma's overweening arrogance, the Creator whose inflated ego threatened the very foundations of creation.

Bhairava was born naked but for a garland of skulls, armed with the dread trident, His skin black as midnight storm-clouds, His eyes flashing with the inevitable reality of annihilation.

Bhairava's presence was an unanswerable question: what is the meaning of your lineage and your status as 'Creator' when faced with the power of Time and Destruction?

106

Homage to the Divine Healer

Om Vaidyāya Namaḥ

Father Brahma, believing himself to be protected by his titles and the deference of the cosmos, was stunned.

He commanded the fearful entity to stand down, invoking his status as the Grandfather of the Worlds.

Bhairava did not argue. He did not seek approval. He simply acted.

With one decisive stroke, he severed one of Father Brahma's five heads.

The blood that flowed was the purging of a persistent illusion: the illusion that his titles and his accolades granted him immunity to the Cosmic Law.

The Divine Father, in His fierce form as Bhairava, proved that the ultimate act of protection is sometimes the destructive one—the eradication of the ego that threatens the whole.

Baba Bhairava, the Guardian, became the great equaliser.

By holding the skull of Brahma the Creator, He became the supreme symbol that in the face of cosmic truth, all lineage, all status, and all claims of inherited power are rendered meaningless.

The protection of the divine family and the cosmos it sustains relies on the cold, hard certainty that the law is absolute.

Bhairava is the one who carries out that truth, embodying the Father who demands discipline and order over all sentimentality and status.

107

I Bow to the Source of All Creation

Om Prabhavē Namaḥ

I knew, however, that even divine justice casts its own shadow of consequence.

For the crime of severing Brahma's fifth head, the skull *Kapala* adhered instantly and immovably to Bhairava's hand.

Bhairava entered His own, terrifying form of *tapasya*. His journey was one of cleansing and purging the sin incurred by the necessity of divine violence.

This was the cosmic price: the enforcer of the law must also submit to its own laws.

Bhairava was cursed to wander the universe as a beggar, perpetually carrying the empty, bleeding vessel of Brahma's pride.

As the Skull-Bearer, the *Kapalika*, Bhairava visited every sacred shrine in the three worlds and yet the curse remained.

He travelled as an outsider, the dark reflection of the Ash-Smeared Yogi, a vagrant figure whose dreadful appearance drove away all but the most fearless devotees.

His penance was the eternal, dynamic confirmation of the law he enforced.

By begging with the head of the Creator, Bhairava continuously taught that even the highest title is temporary and ends in the bone of the skull. He

showed that no one, not even the Divine Father Himself, is above the consequences of karma.

This wandering established Him as the protector of those on the margins. He became the patron of the outcast, the graveyard meditator, the destroyer of the delusion that lineage offers safety.

Bhairava became the living testament that true authority is found not in a throne or in a crown, but in the unshakeable will to uphold the Living Truth, even if it means eternal wandering and self-imposed austerity.

108

Homage to the All-Pervading Lord

Om Viṣṇvē Namaḥ

At the end of his protracted penance, Bhairava arrived before death's own doorway, the flaming ground where the mortal is unmade and the eternal is unveiled.

As Bhairava crossed the sacred threshold to Kashi, the skull of Brahma, long stuck to his hand, shuddered, released its grip, and dropped to the ground.

When the skull detached from his palm and touched Kashi's earth, the burden of sin that had shadowed him everywhere evaporated. Its corrosive stain dissipated, absolving him of his aeon-long sentence.

Freed from the offence, the accompanying darkness retreated, severing the sin for all eternity.

Thus did his penance end, not in death, but in the dawning of deathlessness.

Even though his contrition was complete, his purpose was not, for he was now bound eternally to the guardianship of Kashi.

No one may enter or leave the holy city without first being judged by Him, for Bhairava abides there eternally as its ageless and immortal guardian.

The birth of Bhairava established that even the most justified acts of violence incur a karmic debt, but that the stain of sin is not eternal. It is resolved through penance and purification.

Kashi continues to stand as a living testament to this supreme salvific law.

The site of the absolution became a holy precinct, designated to absorb and purify the final residue of all sin. The script of its salvation folds into the city's own stonework—each step compressing prior moments into the path ahead, securing justice without announcement or appeal.

Bhairava took his position as the supreme guru of cosmic ethics, enforcing Parvati's lesson that the value of the soul is determined not by its birthright, but by the purification earned through its own *tapasya*.

Our story ends here only to begin again. For such is the eternal geometry of the world.

Beware, gods and mortals, of the hubris of your own ego—for it hungers to enthrone itself where equanimity should dwell.

Turn your gaze inwards and purify the obscuration *anava mala* of separation.

What endures is Shiva alone.

Om.

Acknowledgements

Om Namah Shivaya. Om Bhairavaya Namah.

About the Author

Dipa Sanatani is a Singaporean author and the founder of Twinn Swan, an independent publishing house dedicated to Modern Sacred Literature. Through her body of work, Sanatani invites readers into a literary universe where spirituality, philosophy and the sacred converge.

Across more than a dozen books, she writes at the confluence of Hindu thought, world wisdom traditions, and the universal longing for transcendence. Her narratives bridge cultures and faiths, reflecting a cosmopolitan devotion to the idea that all paths—however diverse—lead toward a shared truth. Through myth, history, and introspective storytelling, she contemplates the mysteries of destiny, divinity, and the timeless dialogue between soul and world.

She holds a Bachelor of Commerce and a Bachelor of Arts (Media and Communication) from the University of Melbourne, complemented by a distinguished study abroad program at the Hebrew

University of Jerusalem. Her diverse global experiences—marked by academic pursuit and professional immersion across Japan, China, Australia, and Israel—have enriched her worldview, positioning her as a unique voice within contemporary sacred literature.